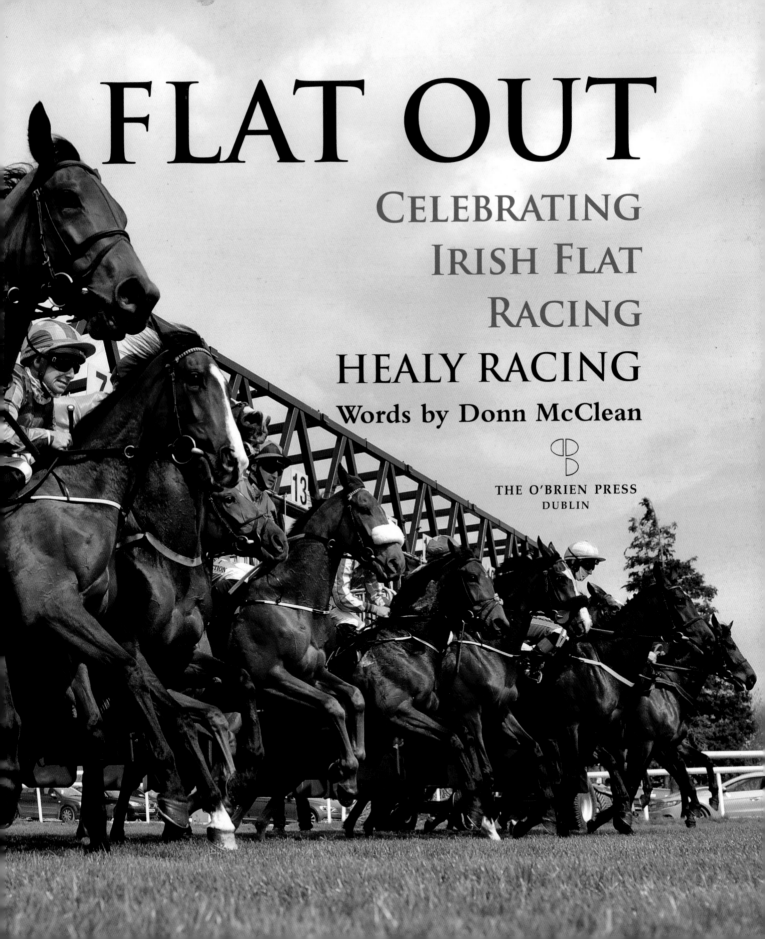

FLAT OUT

CELEBRATING IRISH FLAT RACING

HEALY RACING

Words by Donn McClean

THE O'BRIEN PRESS
DUBLIN

First published in 2021 by The O'Brien Press Ltd,
12 Terenure Road East, Rathgar,
Dublin 6, D06 HD27, Ireland.
Tel: +353 1 4923333; Fax: +353 1 4922777
E-mail: books@obrien.ie
Website: www.obrien.ie
The O'Brien Press is a member of Publishing Ireland.

ISBN: 978-1-78849-278-2

**Healy Racing would like it noted that any horses or riders shown falling
in the following photographs were fine after their spills.**

10 9 8 7 6 5 4 3 2 1
24 23 22 21

Cover and internal design by Emma Byrne.
Layout and design: The O'Brien Press Ltd.
Printed by EDELVIVES, Spain.
This book is produced using pulp from managed forests.

Cover photographs:

Front: Action at Dundalk: *Baby Bellini* and Danny Sheehy (near side), *Banjo* and Annalise Cullen, *Dande* and Martin Clarke (part hidden) with *Dazzling Darren* and Donagh O'Connor (far side).

Back (from top left): Racing in front of the new stand at The Curragh on Irish Derby day, 2019; Investec Derby winner's enclosure at Epsom, 2014, with *Australia* and Joseph O'Brien (in purple silks); They're off in the Breeders' Cup at Keeneland in Kentucky, 2020; Action at Laytown beach, 2018.

Previous page: And they're off! The runners break from starting stalls in the 2021 GAIN The Advantage Series Handicap at Cork.

Published in

DUBLIN
UNESCO
City of Literature

Racing photographer supremo **Pat 'Cash' Healy** is known to many in the horse-racing world. His father Liam senior began the family horse-racing photography business in the 1970s. Today Pat Healy and the other members of the HEALY RACING team, including his brother Liam, his nephews, Kevin and Sean, and his son, Jack, are familiar figures at racetracks around the country and at the big race meetings abroad. From following trainers, horses, owners and jockeys, HEALY RACING has captured thousands of precious moments in the great sport of horse racing, many of which can be viewed on their website healyracing.ie.

One of the go-to experts in the horse-racing world, **Donn McClea**n is an award-winning journalist and author. A three-time nominee for the Horserace Writers' and Photographers' Association's (HWPA) Racing Writer of the Year Award in the UK, his expert reputation has led him to ghostwrite four racing autobiographies, most recently that of twenty-time champion jockey Sir Anthony McCoy. He writes columns on racing for *The Sunday Times* and *The Irish Field*, is a regular guest on Racing TV and RTÉ, and shares his extensive knowledge on his website donnmcclean.com.

Going for home at
The Curragh.

INTRODUCTION

The beauty of a horse is unrivalled. The majesty of a horse at rest, the strength of his stature, the ease of his poise. The speed of a horse at full flight, the fluency of his stride, the power of his gait.

The HEALY RACING team have been capturing horses on camera for decades. Established in the 1970s by Liam Healy, the doyen of horse-racing photographers, HEALY RACING has become a leading provider of racing photographs to the media in Ireland and further afield.

The HEALY RACING team has grown and developed over the years – over the generations – from Liam and his wife, Joan, who started it all in the 1970s out of their family home in Listowel in County Kerry, to now include their children Pat, Liam junior, Cathy and Lisa, and also their grandchildren Jack, Seán, Kevin, Siun and Ruth. The team of contributors has expanded beyond the family confines, and includes Jane Hurley, Stephen O'Doherty, Paul Porter, Aidan Dullaghan, Dan Abraham and Noel Breen.

It is this team that has traversed the world over the course of the last decade, compiling the compendium of flat-racing photographs that have been brought together in these pages. With the depth of material that was available, the primary difficulty lay in choosing which photographs to include and which to leave out. The objective was to capture a cross-section of photographs that represent the vagaries and the nuances of horse racing, as well as the achievements of horses, riders and trainers over the course of the last decade.

This is not a comprehensive account. It is not a narrative of the flat-racing decade. Instead, each picture represents a moment: an expression, a gesture, an achievement. Euphoria in victory, agony in defeat. Angst and anguish, joy and jubilation. Big races, well-known faces, famous moments, as well as horses and occasions and people who may not be so well known. Each instant captured on camera, and a story behind every single one.

Renowned horse-racing writer Donn McClean has provided the words to each picture, a description of an incident or a synopsis of the story that goes with it. The hope is that, together, the pictures and the words will bring the reader on a unique and memorable journey through a remarkable decade of flat racing.

2011

Joseph O'Brien drives *St Nicholas Abbey* to victory at Churchill Downs in the Grade 1 Breeders' Cup Turf, from *Sea Wave* and *Brilliant Speed*.

Above: The Aidan O'Brien-trained *So You Think*, under Ryan Moore, a short-priced winner of the Tattersalls Gold Cup at The Curragh. **Below:** *Balmont Mast* and Ben Curtis are still in front in the five-furlong Racing at Tipperary Maiden, when the horse ducks to his left and crashes through the inside rail, leaving the way clear for *Rose Bonheur* and Declan McDonogh (left) to keep on well to get home by three parts of a length from *Marvada* and Shane Foley (centre).

Right: On the winners' podium, from left, former England cricket captain Michael Vaughan, winning owner David Keoghan, his wife Cecelia Ahern, winning trainer James 'Fozzy' Stack and winning rider Wayne Lordan, after *Lolly For Dolly* has won the Group 2 Windsor Forest Stakes at Royal Ascot.

Below: The Jim Bolger-trained *Banimpire* (near side) stays on strongly for Kevin Manning to get home by a short head from *Field Of Miracles* and Richard Hughes, to land the Group 2 Ribblesdale Stakes at Royal Ascot.

Ningaloo Reef rears and unseats rider Ben Curtis before the start of the Anglo Printers Three-Year-Olds' maiden at Dundalk. Both horse and rider were fine and they took part in the race, finishing ninth.

A 1-2-3 in the Dubai Duty Free Irish Derby for Aidan O'Brien: *Treasure Beach* and
Colm O'Donoghue win by three parts of a length from *Seville* (white face) and
Seamie Heffernan, with *Memphis Tennessee* and Joseph O'Brien (dark silks) taking
third place, a neck in front of the Queen's horse *Carlton House* and Ryan Moore (red
sleeves), with *Dunboyne Express* (noseband in behind) and Declan McDonogh keeping
on to take fifth place.

The horses tread a path between hay bales and sheep at Roscommon, in the Irish Stallion Farms EBF Maiden, won by the Ger Lyons-trained *Lightening Pearl*, under Johnny Murtagh, who is just showing in front (partially obscured), from *Among Equals* and Colm O'Donoghue. Two months later, *Lightening Pearl* won the Group 3 Round Tower Stakes at The Curragh, and a month after that, Ger Lyons sent the *Marju* filly to Newmarket for the Group 1 Cheveley Park Stakes and, ridden again by Johnny Murtagh, she got home by three parts of a length from *Sunday Times*, to provide trainer Ger Lyons with his first Group 1 win.

They head away from the stands with just under a circuit to run at Ballinrobe, County Mayo, as the cattle and sheep remain completely uninterested.

Pat Smullen salutes as he passes the post in front on the Dermot Weld-trained *Emulous* in the Group 1 Coolmore Fusaichi Pegasus Matron Stakes at Leopardstown, clear of *Together* and Colm O'Donoghue (purple cap), *Misty For Me* and Seamie Heffernan (striped cap), *Barefoot Lady* and Tony Hamilton (blue cap) and *Wild Wind* and Joseph O'Brien (navy cap).

Left: Jockey Johnny Murtagh with Jacqueline O'Brien in the winner's enclosure at The Curragh after he has ridden *Bewitched*, trained by Jacqueline O'Brien's son Charles and owned by Jacqueline with her daughter Susan, to victory in the Group 3 Renaissance Stakes.

Below: Rider Declan McDonogh is in the zone as he guides the Patrick Prendergast-trained *Coral Wave* to an impressive victory in the Listed Flame Of Tara EBF Stakes at The Curragh for owner Rick Barnes.

Joseph O'Brien receives a congratulatory kiss from his mother
Annemarie after he has ridden *St Nicholas Abbey*, trained by
his father Aidan, to victory in the Breeders' Cup Turf. Aged
eighteen years and 166 days, he became the youngest rider
ever to win a Breeders' Cup race, and he and his dad Aidan
became the first father and son to team up as trainer and
rider and win a Breeders' Cup race.

2012

The runners leave the back straight and turn for home in the Crowne Plaza Hotel Dundalk Handicap at Dundalk.

Above: In the winner's enclosure with *Camelot* after he has won the Dubai Duty Free Irish Derby are, from left, Sarah O'Brien, Ana O'Brien, groom David Hickey, rider Joseph O'Brien, trainer Aidan O'Brien, Annemarie O'Brien and Donnacha O'Brien.

Opposite top: *Camelot* in full flow on the gallops at Ballydoyle with Kaname Tsuge.

Opposite bottom: The Aidan O'Brien-trained *Camelot* and rider Joseph O'Brien return to the winner's enclosure at Epsom, having won the Investec Derby, the first time ever that a father and son teamed up as trainer and jockey to win the Derby.

Above: Rider Martin Harley (left) and trainer Mick Channon (right) are all smiles in the winner's enclosure with *Samitar* and groom Abid Hussain after they have won the Irish 1000 Guineas.

Left: The John Murphy-trained *Gossamer Seed* pricks her ears as she goes clear under Shane Foley in the Group 3 Athasi Stakes.

Dandy Boy with trainer David Marnane (left) and groom
James Casey (right) in the winner's enclosure at Royal Ascot
after winning the Wokingham Handicap.

ROYAL ASCOT

Above: Rider Ryan Moore eases down on *Simenon* after passing the winning post six lengths clear of their closest pursuer in the Ascot Stakes at Royal Ascot as, afterwards (**left**), winning trainer Willie Mullins doffs his (top) hat on the winners' podium.

The Andy Oliver-trained *Sendmylovetorose* keeps on well for Colm O'Donoghue to win the Group 2 Cherry Hinton Stakes at Newmarket, with *Jadanna* (number 4) finishing third under Frankie Dettori.

Left: President Higgins and *Great Heavens* both look surprised in the winner's enclosure at The Curragh after the John Gosden-trained filly has won the Darley Irish Oaks under William Buick.

Below: Pictured before the Ladies Derby Handicap at The Curragh are riders (back row, left to right) Aine O'Connor, Marta Pisarek, Serena Stack, Sarah Lynam, Adrienne Foley, Jane Mangan, (front row, left to right) Danielle Quinlan, Kate Harrison, Katie Walsh and Nina Carberry. The race was won by the Richard Brabazon-trained *Placere*, who was ridden to victory by Nina Carberry.

The John Oxx-trained *Saddler's Rock* stays on strongly under Johnny Murtagh (yellow and red hooped cap), running out an impressive winner of the Group 2 Goodwood Cup.

Above: The Sir Henry Cecil-trained *Chachamaidee* and Tom Queally (near side, yellow cap) swoop down the outside of *Duntle* and Wayne Lordan (centre, white cap) and *Emulous* and Pat Smullen (far side, pink cap) in the Group 1 Coolmore Fusaichi Pegasus Matron Stakes at Leopardstown. *Duntle* got to the winning line a short head in front of *Chachamaideee*, with *Emulous* a half a length back in third but, after a stewards' enquiry, the placings of the first two were reversed, with *Chachamaideee* awarded the race. She was Sir Henry Cecil's final Group 1 winner in Ireland.

Opposite top: *Snow Fairy* (number 3, near side) and Frankie Dettori go toe-to-toe with *Nathaniel* and William Buick in the Red Mills Irish Champion Stakes at Leopardstown. In the end, the Ed Dunlop-trained filly, *Snow Fairy*, got home by just over a length from John Gosden's *Nathaniel* and, afterwards (**opposite bottom**), *Snow Fairy* and Frankie Dettori share a moment in the winner's enclosure.

Above: Trainer Tommy Carmody shakes rider Niall McCullagh's hand after *Royal Diamond's* win in the Gain Horse Feeds Irish St Leger.

Opposite: *Dawn Approach* and Kevin Manning pull up and start to make their way back to the winner's enclosure after they have won the Group 1 Dubai Dewhurst Stakes at Newmarket. It was the fifth win in the race in seven years for the rider and for *Dawn Approach's* trainer Jim Bolger.

2013

They're off on Breeders'
Cup day at Santa Anita in
California!

In the winner's enclosure after *Dawn Approach* won the Qipco 2000 Guineas at Newmarket,
(from left) Úna Manning, winning trainer and breeder Jim Bolger, Jackie Bolger, Clare Manning,
travelling head lad Ger Flynn, James Manning and winning rider Kevin Manning.

'Look how much I won!' Michael Murphy, cousin of trainer Joe Murphy, showing his winning ticket to the trainer's son Joe Murphy Jnr and owner Tom Egan after *Euphrasia* has sprung a 33/1 surprise in the Group 3 Blue Wind Stakes at Naas.

Above: Rider Joseph O'Brien eases down at the line on the Aidan O'Brien-trained *Magician*, clear of his stable companion *Gale Force Ten*, in the Irish 2000 Guineas.

Left: *Just The Judge* in the winner's enclosure after winning the Etihad Airways Irish 1000 Guineas, with (from left) rider Jamie Spencer alongside Sheikh Fahad Al Thani and Ben Sangster of joint owners Qatar Racing and the Sangster Family respectively.

Left: In the winner's enclosure after *Sole Power* had won the King's Stand Stakes at Royal Ascot are owners David and Sabena Power (centre) together with their sons Willie (second from left) and Paddy (right), their daughters-in-law Ruth Chamberlain (left) and Tessa Power (third from right), and trainer Eddie Lynam's daughters Amy (third from left) and Sarah (second from right).

Below: *Dawn Approach* and Kevin Manning (left, blue cap) get the better of *Toronado* and Richard Hughes (grey cap) in a thrilling finish to the St James's Palace Stakes at Royal Ascot. It was a big performance by the Jim Bolger-trained colt, the Guineas winner bouncing back to form just seventeen days after he had finished last in the Derby.

2013

Joseph O'Brien drives *St Nicholas Abbey* to victory in the Investec Coronation Cup at Epsom. It was a record third victory in the race for the Aidan O'Brien-trained horse.

Hats in the air in the Royal Ascot winner's enclosure for members of the
Roca Tumu Syndicate after their horse, *Roca Tumu*, ridden by Billy Lee (fourth
from left) and trained by Joanna Morgan, has landed the Britannia Handicap.

Trading Leather stays on strongly under Kevin Manning to land the Irish Derby. It was a first Irish Derby for the rider, and a second for trainer Jim Bolger, who also bred *Trading Leather*, twenty-one years after he won his first with *St Jovite*.

Chicquita and Johnny Murtagh on their way to the start before winning the Darley Irish Oaks. *Chicquita* was sold for €6 million at Goffs the following November.

Busted Tycoon goes clear under Fran Berry to win the Caulfieldindustrial. com Handicap at the Galway Festival. It was the first of a hat-trick of wins for the Tony Martin-trained mare during the week, on her way to becoming the first horse to win three times at the same Galway Festival.

Opposite: Connor King makes a valiant, but ultimately unsuccessful, effort to keep the partnership intact as *Wordsaplenty* rears before the start of the John O'Connor Engineering Handicap at Killarney. Thankfully, both horse and rider emerged from the incident unscathed.

Below: Wayne Lordan drives the David Wachman-trained *Sudirman* (second from right) to victory in the Phoenix Stakes at The Curragh, from *Big Time* and Pat Smullen (right) and *War Command* and Joseph O'Brien (left). It was the second Group 1 win of the rider's career, three years after his first with the 100/1 shot *Sole Power* in the Coolmore Nunthorpe Stakes at York.

Rider Johnny Murtagh shakes hands with joint-owner Morgan Cahalan in the
winner's enclosure at Haydock, after he has ridden the Tom Hogan-trained *Gordon
Lord Byron* to victory in the Betfred Sprint Cup. The win turned out to be Johnny
Murtagh's final Group 1 victory as a rider.

The John Gosden-trained filly *The Fugue* and William Buick (left) come wide into the home straight before unleashing a run that takes her past *Al Kazeem* and James Doyle (blue and white quartered cap) and *Trading Leather* and Kevin Manning (purple and white checked cap) and on to victory in the Red Mills Irish Champion Stakes at Leopardstown.

Group I double! **Below:** Chris Hayes drives the Kevin Prendergast-trained *La Collina* home in the Coolmore Fusaichi Pegasus Matron Stakes at Leopardstown, a first Group I win for the rider and, eight days later (**opposite**), the rider celebrates as he returns to the winner's enclosure after recording his second Group I win on the Dermot Weld-trained *Voleuse De Coeurs* in the Irish St Leger at The Curragh.

Opposite top: Jockeys' Corner: Champion flat jockeys at Limerick to support JT McNamara and Jonjo Bright (from left): Kieren Fallon, Johnny Murtagh, Declan McDonogh, Tom Queally, Joseph O'Brien, Jamie Spencer and Pat Smulen.

Opposite bottom: Declan McDonogh drives the Barry Lalor-trained *Maarek* (near side, noseband) home in the Group 1 Qatar Prix de l'Abbaye de Longchamp, a short neck in front of François-Xavier Bertras on *Catcall*.

Above: The Paul Deegan-trained *Sruthan* stays on well for Chris Hayes to get home by three parts of a length from *Big Break* and Pat Smullen in the Group 3 Coolmore Home Of Champions Concorde Stakes at Tipperary.

51

2014

The May scene after morning gallops under the trees at Aidan O'Brien's Ballydoyle stables, with *Australia* (chestnut with white blaze) in centre.

Owner John Magnier shakes rider Ryan Moore's hand in the winner's enclosure at The Curragh after *Marvellous*'s win in the Irish 1000 Guineas, as groom Maria Gray looks on.

Kingman and James Doyle (pink cap) come clear of *Shifting Power* and Richard Hughes (purple sleeves) and *Mustajeeb* and Pat Smullen (blue sleeves) to win the Irish 2000 Guineas by five lengths at The Curragh.

The Eddie Lynam-trained *Sole Power* quickens up smartly under Richard Hughes in the King's Stand Stakes at Royal Ascot and gets home by over a length from *Stepper Point* (number 10) and *Hot Streak* (maroon silks).

Above: *Domination* and rider Fran Berry in the winner's enclosure at Royal Ascot after the pair of them have won the Ascot Stakes, flanked by, from left, John O'Gorman, Cora Byrnes, owner Martin Whyte, groom Keith Sous and trainer Charles Byrnes.

Left: Grooms Paddy 'Whacker' O'Brien and Caroline Cashman with the Dermot Weld-trained *Mustajeeb* in the winner's enclosure after Pat Smullen has ridden him to victory in the Jersey Stakes at Royal Ascot.

Leading Light and Joseph O'Brien (right) stays on strongly
to win the Gold Cup at Royal Ascot from the Queen's filly
Estimate (centre, noseband) under Ryan Moore, and the
Michael Winters-trained *Missunited* (left) and Jim Crowley.

Opposite top: It's two on the board so far for trainer Eddie Lynam at Royal Ascot, with *Anthem Alexander* winning the Queen Mary Stakes a day after *Sole Power* had won the King's Stand Stakes (for the second consecutive year). Three days later, it was three, with *Slade Power* running out an impressive winner of the Diamond Jubilee Stakes.

Opposite bottom: Owners David and Sabena Power are congratulated by Queen Elisabeth II after *Slade Power* wins the Diamond Jubilee Stakes at Royal Ascot.

Below: Ryan Moore drives Willie Mullins' grey horse *Pique Sous* to victory in the Queen Alexandra Stakes, the final race of Royal Ascot 2014.

Above: *Australia*, again under Joseph O'Brien, follows up his Epsom win by easily winning the Irish Derby at The Curragh, from stable companions *Kingfisher* and *Orchestra*, providing trainer Aidan O'Brien with a 1-2-3 in the race.

Opposite top: *Australia* and Joseph O'Brien (purple cap) get the better of *Kingston Hill* and Andrea Atzeni (navy cap) to land the Epsom Derby. It was a third Epsom Derby in a row for trainer Aidan O'Brien, and a fifth in total.

Opposite bottom: Derby winner's enclosure: Joseph O'Brien is the one in the purple silks, MV Magnier is the one in the orange tie, and *Australia* is the one with the long face!

Bracelet stretches out her head willingly for Colm O'Donoghue to get home by a neck from her stable companion *Tapestry* (near side), ridden by Joseph O'Brien on a 'postage stamp' saddle, and the Luca Cumani-trained *Volume* (far side) in the Irish Oaks, giving her trainer Aidan O'Brien his fourth Irish Oaks, and rider Colm O'Donoghue his first.

Missunited and Jim Crowley get home by a half a length in the Group 3 Lillie Langtry Stakes at Goodwood from *Arabian Comet* (noseband, far side) who runs on to take second place from *Waila* (blinkers, near side). It was the Michael Winters-trained filly's final run on the racecourse, and she went out on a high, 364 days after she had won the Galway Hurdle at the Galway Festival.

It's all very tight as *Sole Power* and Richard Hughes (red and white checked cap) burst through between *Hot Streak* (noseband, eventual fifth) and *Moviesta* (right, eventual fourth) to land the Nunthorpe Stakes at York. It was a second win in the race for the Eddie Lynam-trained horse, four years after he had sprung a 100/1 shock as a three-year-old in 2010.

Above: Groom Valerie Keatley leads in *Mutual Regard* as Louis Steward celebrates after he has guided the Johnny Murtagh-trained horse to victory in the Ebor at York – the oldest and probably most famous race at York and the richest flat handicap in Europe.

Opposite: *Arbitrageur* and Johnny King flying high at Laytown as groom Aidan Wall looks on.

Donnacha O'Brien returns to the winner's enclosure at Dundalk after landing the Dundalk Stadium Apprentice Maiden on *Quartz* – the first winner of his riding career.

They wheel around the home turn in the Qipco Irish Champion Stakes, with *The Grey Gatsby* (grey horse, second from right) and Ryan Moore just about to make a move that will see them catch and pass *Australia* and Joseph O'Brien (purple cap, left) close home in a thriller. Also in the picture are (left to right) *Al Kazeem* (eventual fifth), *Mukhadram* (fourth), *Trading Leather* (third), *Kingfisher* (sixth) and *Alkasser* (seventh).

Trainer Willie McCreery congratulates rider Billy Lee as he returns
to Leopardstown's winner's enclosure on *Fiesolana*, after winning the
Coolmore Fastnet Rock Matron Stakes. It was a first Group 1 win for
both trainer and rider.

The Sabrina Harty-trained *Ansgar* keeps on well for James Doyle (pink and black cap) to hold off the challenge of eventual third, *Gregorian*, and William Buick (green cap) in the Group 2 OLBG Park Stakes at Doncaster, with *Aljamaaheer* and Paul Hanagan (blue and white striped cap) running on to take second place.

A worm's-eye view of *Brown Panther* and Richard Kingscote, as they coast to
victory in the Palmerstown House Estate Irish St Leger.

The Aidan O'Brien-trained *Found* and Ryan Moore power to victory in the Prix Marcel Boussac at Longchamp from *Ervedya* and Christophe Soumillon.

2015

The sun sets on Down Royal as riders make their way down to the start for the concluding race at the May meeting.

The David Wachman-trained *Legatissimo* stays on strongly under Ryan Moore (striped cap)
to get the better of *Lucida* and Kevin Manning in the Qipco 1000 Guineas at Newmarket.

Gleneagles (centre) quickens up well for Ryan Moore, between *Endless Drama* (near side) and *Ivawood* (far side), to land the Tattersalls Irish 2000 Guineas.

The Moyglare Stud's colt *Free Eagle* wins the Prince of Wales's Stakes at Royal Ascot under a brilliant ride by Pat Smullen, who dictated the early fractions to suit Dermot Weld's horse, but kept enough in reserve to fend off the late lunge of *The Grey Gatsby* under Jamie Spencer.

Clondaw Warrior in the winner's enclosure at Royal Ascot after winning the
Ascot Stakes, with members of owners, the Act D Wagg Syndicate: (from left)
Gillian Walsh, Aisling Gannon, Áine Casey and Tamso Cox.

Number One! William Buick returns to the winner's enclosure at The Curragh, having won the Irish Derby on the Godolphin colt *Jack Hobbs*. The John Gosden-trained colt was the first English-trained winner of the Irish Derby since Pat Eddery had driven the Henry Cecil-trained *Commander In Chief* to victory in 1993.

The Hugo Palmer-trained *Covert Love* runs out an impressive winner of the Darley Irish Oaks under Pat Smullen, from *Jack Naylor* (right, noseband) and *Curvy* (centre).

The ladies on Ladies' Day at the Galway Races!

Above: The Jim Bolger-trained *Pleascach* stays on best of all under Kevin Manning (blue cap) to get home in a thrilling finish to the Darley Yorkshire Oaks from *Covert Love* (number 3, near side), *Sea Calisi* (far side) and *Curvy* (number 5).

Opposite: Frankie Dettori is flying high after winning the Lonsdale Cup at York on *Max Dynamite*, as owner Rich Ricci celebrates.

Close to the action on the beach at Laytown in County Meath.

Opposite: The David Wachman-trained *Legatissimo* keeps on well for Wayne Lordan to land the Matron Stakes at Leopardstown.

Below: The John Gosden-trained *Golden Horn* veers to his right as they race inside the final 200 yards of the Irish Champion Stakes at Leopardstown, colliding with *Free Eagle*. *Golden Horn* and Frankie Dettori (red cap) were first past the post, with *Found* and Seamie Heffernan (blue cap) staying on well to take second place in front of *Free Eagle* and Pat Smullen (red cap with black star). The stewards held an enquiry into the incident, but the placings were left unaltered.

Order Of St George and Joseph O'Brien go clear in the Irish St Leger, extending their lead to 11 lengths by the time they get to the winning line. Aidan O'Brien's horse was the first three-year-old to win the Irish St Leger since Vinnie Roe won the first of his four in 2001. This was also Joseph O'Brien's final Group 1 win as a rider.

FLAT OUT

Below: *Sole Power* and Chris Hayes (red and white checked cap) just hold on from *Maarek* and Jamie Spencer (white cap) to land the Derrinstown Stud Flying Five Stakes at The Curragh.

Opposite top: The Dermot Weld-trained *Fascinating Rock* gets home in the Champion Stakes at Ascot under a determined drive from Pat Smullen, with *Found* and Ryan Moore (striped cap) chasing him home.

Opposite bottom: Trainer Aidan O'Brien looks on as *Found* pricks her ears under Michael Hussey on a sunny morning at Keeneland in Kentucky before competing in the Breeders' Cup Turf, in which she came out best at the end of a protracted duel with *Golden Horn*.

2016

Sunset at Dundalk and the
light shines through for
Ross Coakley and *Untapped
Spectrum* …

Chris Hayes celebrates as he and the Kevin Prendergast-trained
Awtaad cross the line in the Irish 2000 Guineas, clear of the
Newmarket Guineas winner *Galileo Gold*.

Jet Setting and Shane Foley (black cap) get the better of *Minding* and Ryan Moore in a thrilling conclusion to the Irish 1000 Guineas. It was a first Group 1 win for rider Shane Foley and for *Jet Setting*'s trainer Adrian Keatley.

FLAT OUT

Ryan Moore punches Irish 1000 Guineas winner *Minding* out to an impressive victory in the Sea The Stars Pretty Polly Stakes at The Curragh, with *Bocca Baciata* and *Lucida* chasing her home.

Left: Pat Smullen punches the air just after he crosses the line on *Harzand* in the Epsom Derby, the fulfillment of a long-held ambition for the rider and for the colt's trainer Dermot Weld.

Below: *Harzand* and Pat Smullen (far side) get the better of a terrific duel with *Idaho* and Seamie Heffernan to land the Irish Derby at The Curragh.

Members of the *Jennies Jewel* party in the winner's enclosure at Royal Ascot after Ronan Whelan had ridden the Jarlath Fahey-trained mare to victory in the Ascot Stakes.

Trainer Michael Halford and rider James Doyle on the winner's podium at Royal Ascot after *Portage* had won the Royal Hunt Cup.

Order Of St George and Ryan Moore coast to victory in the Gold Cup at Royal Ascot,
a record-breaking seventh Gold Cup for trainer Aidan O'Brien.

Adam Kirby celebrates as he guides *Commissioned* to victory in the Queen Alexandra Stakes, a first Royal Ascot winner for *Commissioned*'s trainer Gordon Elliott.

And they're off at Dundalk! *Zorba The Greek* (second from left) rears a little as Declan McDonogh sits tight. Charles O'Brien's horse was beaten a short head in the end by the Johnny Feane-trained *Park Row* (not in picture).

Declan McDonogh and the Andrew Slattery-trained *Creggs
Pipes* are clear around the home turn on their way to
winning the Colm Quinn BMW Mile at Galway.

That puts the hat on it! Trainer Tony Martin celebrates in the winner's enclosure after *Heartbreak City* has won the Ebor at York with (from left) Niall Reilly, a member of owners the Here For The Craic Syndicate, winning rider Adam McNamara, *Heartbreak City*, and groom Cathy O'Leary. A month earlier, *Heartbreak City* had won a handicap hurdle at Galway. Three months later, he went to Australia and was beaten by a head in the Melbourne Cup.

Toni Fidgeon, wearing the Michael Tabor silks, points out her parents in the crowd to Frankie Dettori, also wearing the Michael Tabor silks (blue, orange disk, striped sleeves), before the Irish Champion Stakes at Leopardstown. Frankie Dettori rode *Found* in the race, who finished second, beaten a half a length by *Almanzor,* ridden by Christophe Soumillon, pictured in the Ecurie Antonio Caro silks (light blue with navy spots). Toni Fidgeon didn't have a ride in the race.

Irish Champion Stakes winner *Almanzor*, out on his own, with Christophe Soumillon on board. Jean-Claude Rouget's horse was the first French-trained winner of the Irish Champion Stakes since the John Hammond-trained *Suave Dancer* won the race in 1991.

Donnacha O'Brien (red cap) drives *Intricately* – trained by his brother Joseph – home in the Moyglare Stud Stakes at The Curragh, just getting the better of Padraig Beggy and *Hydrangea*, trained by the boys' dad Aidan. It was a first Group 1 winner as a trainer for Joseph O'Brien, and a first Group 1 winner as a rider for Donnacha O'Brien.

Left: Rider Frankie Dettori and trainer Willie Mullins share a moment in the winner's enclosure at The Curragh after *Wicklow Brave*'s victory in the Irish St Leger.

Below: *Found* and Ryan Moore power to victory in the Prix de l'Arc de Triomphe at Chantilly. Aidan O'Brien's filly was followed home by her stable companions *Highland Reel* and *Order Of St George*, to complete a memorable 1-2-3 for the trainer in one of the most prestigious races in the world.

2017

Turning for home at Dundalk. From right in the front row: Pat Smullen, Chris Hayes, Kevin Manning (white sleeves) and Leigh Roche (yellow sleeves).

Ryan Moore eases down on *Winter* at the winning line in the Irish 1000 Guineas at The Curragh, three weeks after Aidan O'Brien's filly had won the 1000 Guineas at Newmarket under Wayne Lordan.

Churchill and Ryan Moore come clear of *Thunder Moon* and Christophe Soumillon
in the Irish 2000 Guineas at The Curragh.

The Aidan O'Brien-trained *Wings Of Eagles* (near side, number 18) under
Padraig Beggy swoops late to collar his stable companion *Cliffs Of Moher* and
Ryan Moore (navy cap) deep inside the final furlong in the Epsom Derby, with
Cracksman and Frankie Dettori (red cap, partially obscured) back in third.

Thomas Hobson and Ryan Moore are clear at the line in the Ascot Stakes at Royal Ascot. It was the third time in six years that the rider had teamed up with trainer Willie Mullins to land the Ascot Stakes.

The Aidan O'Brien-trained *Capri* (near side, number 1) and Seamie Heffernan just hold
on from *Cracksman* and Pat Smullen (far side, red cap) and *Wings Of Eagles* (number 9)
and Ryan Moore to land the Irish Derby, in front of the temporary stand at The Curragh.

Frankie Dettori comes back in after easily winning the Irish Oaks on the
John Gosden-trained *Enable*.

The Joe Murphy-trained *Only Mine*, under rider Gary Carroll, runs out an easy winner of the Listed Yeomanstown Stud Dark Angel Stakes at Naas.

Dylan Browne McMonagle (purple and yellow) heading for a win on *I've Got It* in the Sean Cleary Memorial Race at Dingle. With five wins over the three-day event, Dylan was crowned Dingle Champion jockey for the second consecutive year.

Ryan Moore (purple cap) drives the Aidan O'Brien-trained *Capri* to victory in the St Leger at Doncaster, flanked by the yellow-capped pair, Jim Crowley and *Crystal Ocean* (left) and James Doyle and *Stradivarius* (right). This turned out to be one of the strongest renewals of the oldest Classic run in recent years, with *Crystal Ocean* going on to win the Hardwicke Stakes the following year and the Prince of Wales's Stakes the year after that, while *Stradivarius* won the next three renewals of the Ascot Gold Cup. As well as that, the Joseph O'Brien-trained *Rekindling*, who finished fourth here under Donnacha O'Brien (white cap), went to Australia and won the Melbourne Cup two months after the St Leger.

Trainer Roger Charlton with rider Andrea Atzeni in the winner's enclosure at Leopardstown after *Decorated Knight*'s victory in the Irish Champion Stakes.

Stable companions *Rhododendron* (near side) and *Hydrangea* go nose-to-nose through the final stages of the Prix de l'Opera at Chantilly in a 1-2 for trainer Aidan O'Brien, with *Rhododendron* and Seamie Heffernan prevailing by a head.

US Navy Flag and Ryan Moore go clear in the Dewhurst
Stakes at Newmarket, and are chased home by
Mendelssohn, *Seahenge* and *Threeandfourpence* to complete
a 1-2-3-4 for trainer Aidan O'Brien.

Above: The Joseph O'Brien-trained *Rekindling* and Corey Brown (pink cap) swoop late to collar the Aidan O'Brien-trained *Johannes Vermeer* and Ben Melham (navy cap), with the Willie Mullins-trained *Max Dynamite* and Zac Purton (pink cap) back in third, completing a famous 1-2-3 for Irish trainers in 'The Race That Stops a Nation', the Melbourne Cup.

Left: Trainer Joseph O'Brien and rider Corey Brown with the Melbourne Cup after *Rekindling*'s victory.

2018

It's wet and sloppy ahead of The Breeders' Cup at Churchill Downs, Kentucky!

FLAT OUT

Below: The Aidan O'Brien-trained *Saxon Warrior* powers to victory in the 2000 Guineas at Newmarket under Donnacha O'Brien, who was riding his first Classic winner, with subsequent quadruple Group 1 winner *Roaring Lion* (number 12) back in fifth, and subsequent Derby winner *Masar* (chestnut, white blaze) behind in third.

Opposite top: Trainer Ken Condon congratulates Shane Foley after the rider has steered *Romanised* to victory in the Irish 2000 Guineas at The Curragh, a first Classic win for the trainer.

Opposite bottom: Rider Colm O'Donoghue and trainer Jessica Harrington celebrate after *Alpha Centauri*'s victory in the Irish 1000 Guineas at The Curragh, with groom Debbie Flavin (left) and Electra Niarchos (right) of owners the Niarchos Family.

Trainer Aidan O'Brien's second string of the morning heading for the front gallop at Ballydoyle.

On the winners' podium at Royal Ascot (from left) trainer David Marnane, owners Maurice Casey and Denis McGettigan, and rider Billy Lee, after their horse *Settle For Bay* has won the Royal Hunt Cup.

Trainer Jessica Harrington and head man Eamon Leigh in the winner's enclosure at Royal Ascot with *Alpha Centauri* after their filly had put up a pulsating performance in winning the Coronation Stakes by six lengths.

Trainer Joseph O'Brien with his brother and rider Donnacha in
the winner's enclosure at The Curragh after the pair of them
teamed up with *Latrobe* to land the Irish Derby.

The Aidan O'Brien-trained *Kew Gardens* stretches out nicely under Ryan Moore to land the Grand Prix de Paris at Longchamp, beating *Neufbosc* by just over a length.

They're off in the qualified riders' race at Bellewstown, with the eventual winner, the Ted Walsh-trained *Minnie Dahill* (centre, green hoops), rearing slightly under Jody Townend.

The Roses of Tralee with the jockeys at Killarney.

Melbourne Cup reflections during the promotional tour 2018: Trainer Dermot Weld,
who won the race twice, with *Vintage Crop* in 1993 and *Media Puzzle* in 2002.

Rider James Doyle delivers the William Haggas-trained *Sea Of Class* (near side, number 6) with a perfectly-timed run to get up and beat *Forever Together* (far side, number 2) by a neck in the Irish Oaks at The Curragh.

Smiles all round: Carol Cassidy (centre) is best-dressed at Sligo.

All part of a bigger picture: The Sarah Lynam-trained *Tyrconnell* (far left, red silks) is delivered late by Danny Sheehy to land the final race of the day at Laytown.

Oisín Murphy returns to the winner's enclosure at Leopardstown after
he has ridden the John Gosden-trained *Roaring Lion* to victory in the Irish
Champion Stakes, led in by Sheikh Fahad of owners Qatar Racing (left),
and groom Benario de Pavia.

Above: The Aidan O'Brien-trained *Flag Of Honour* comes clear under Ryan Moore to land the Irish St Leger, chased home by *Latrobe* (number 6) and *Weekender* (number 3) and, afterwards (**below**), a quiet moment together for horse, trainer and rider.

Ronan Whelan is congratulated by weigh-room colleagues, (from left) Conor
Hoban, Colin Keane and Shane Foley, after he has landed the first Group 1 win of
his career on the Patrick Prendergast-trained *Skitter Scatter* in the Moyglare Stud
Stakes at The Curragh.

Riders Chris Hayes (red silks) and Cameron Noble fight for the Ayr Gold Cup,
after they have dead-heated in the race on, respectively, *Son Of Rest*, trained by
Fozzy Stack (third from left), and the Paul Cole-trained *Baron Bolt*.

2019

Sovereign and Padraig Beggy are not for catching in the Irish Derby in front of the packed new grandstand that heralded in a new era for The Curragh.

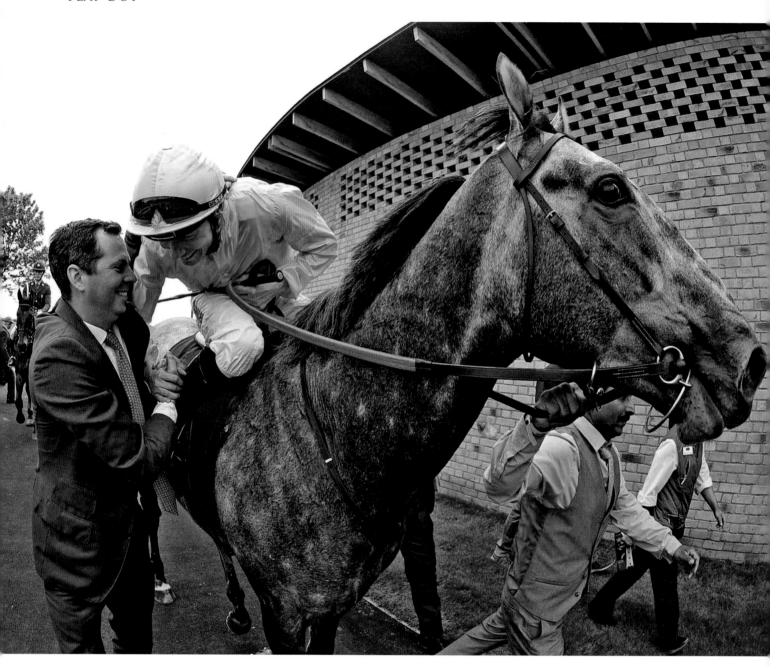

Trainer Charlie Hills congratulates rider Jamie Spencer on *Phoenix Of Spain* on the walk back in from the racecourse to the winner's enclosure at The Curragh after they have won the Irish 2000 Guineas.

Above: Ryan Moore goes clear on the Aidan O'Brien-trained *Hermosa* in the Irish 1000 Guineas, chased home by the Michael Bell-trained *Pretty Pollyanna* and Frankie Dettori (white cap) and the Paddy Twomey-trained *Foxtrot Liv* under Billy Lee (orange cap).

Left: The Aidan O'Brien-trained *Circus Maximus* holds on under Ryan Moore (who has just dropped his whip) from *King Of Comedy* and Adam Kirby (near side) to land the Queen Anne Stakes at Royal Ascot.

2019

The Jessica Harrington-trained *Calling Time* stays on strongly for Shane Foley (black cap) to land the Flesk Handicap at Killarney, in the shadows of Mangerton Mountain.

Frankie Dettori flies high in the winner's enclosure at The Curragh after he has won the Irish Oaks on the John Gosden-trained *Star Catcher*.

There are many with chances as they turn for home in the Connacht Hotel Qualified Riders' Handicap at the Galway Festival, but the eventual winner, the Willie Mullins-trained *Great White Shark*, is taken widest of all by Jody Townend (yellow sleeves) before being delivered with her perfectly-timed winning run up the final climb.

Above: Connections of *One Cool Poet* celebrate in the rain after their horse has recorded his third win of Galway week in the McDonogh Capital Investments Handicap, thereby becoming the first horse to win three times on the flat at the same Galway Festival.

Opposite top: Trainer Ger Lyons and rider Colin Keane in the winner's enclosure with *Siskin* after victory in the Phoenix Stakes at The Curragh, a first domestic Group 1 win for both trainer and rider.

Opposite bottom: It's Ladies' Day at Listowel.

The Charlie Appleby-trained *Pinatubo* is seriously impressive under a
delighted William Buick in winning the National Stakes at The Curragh by
nine lengths.

Chris Hayes has a look around as he lands the Irish St Leger on the
Dermot Weld-trained *Search For A Song*, making her the first three-
year-old filly to win the race in thirty years. It was a remarkable
performance by the Moyglare Stud's filly, given how keenly she ran
through the early stages of the race.

Above: The Aidan O'Brien-trained *Magical* comes clear under Ryan Moore to win the Irish Champion Stakes at Leopardstown, with her stable companions *Magic Wand* (left) and *Anthony Van Dyck* (centre) chasing her home.

Opposite top: Nine-time champion jockey Pat Smullen with twenty-time champion jockey AP McCoy in the winner's enclosure at The Curragh after the Pat Smullen Champions' Race for Cancer Trials Ireland, which AP won on the Sheila Lavery-trained *Quizical*. It was an extraordinary day and an extraordinary race, a race for which nine champion jockeys came out of retirement to compete against each other in a champions' race, with AP McCoy, Ruby Walsh and Johnny Murtagh fighting out the finish. The race was the brainchild of Pat Smullen, and it raised over €2.6 million for cancer research.

Opposite bottom: Andrew Slattery holds his trophy aloft after landing the first Group race win of his career on the Dermot Weld-trained *Kastasa* in the Loughbrown Stakes at The Curragh.

The Jessica Harrington-trained *Millisle* finishes off her race strongly for Shane Foley to land the Cheveley Park Stakes at Newmarket.

The Jessica Harrington-trained *Albigna* goes for home under Shane Foley in the Prix Marcel Boussac at Longchamp, with *Marieta* and *Flighty Lady* giving vain chase.

Magical follows up her Irish Champion Stakes win by landing the Champion Stakes at Ascot under Donnacha O'Brien, getting home by three parts of a length from *Addeybb*. This was Donnacha O'Brien's final Group 1 win as a rider.

Early shades of autumn as they race down the back straight at Gowan Park in County Kilkenny.

2020

Seamie Heffernan (white cap) is brilliant on *Magical*, as Aidan O'Brien's filly gets the better of *Ghaiyyath* in a fascinating Irish Champion Stakes at Leopardstown. On the far left is the 2020 winner of the Prix de l'Arc de Triomphe, *Sottsass*.

Opposite top: At home with Colin Keane, *Siskin* and trainer Ger Lyons.

Opposite bottom: *Siskin* shows a sparkling turn of foot, delivered with perfect timing by rider Colin Keane, to go clear of his rivals deep inside the final furlong of the Irish 2000 Guineas at The Curragh.

Above: *Alpine Star* and Frankie Dettori are clear in the Coronation Stakes in front of an empty grandstand at Royal Ascot.

Racing continues behind closed doors due to Covid-19, with jockeys leaving their temporary changing room in The Arkle Bar at Navan and heading for the parade ring.

Opposite top: *Santiago* and Seamie Heffernan return to the winner's enclosure after landing the Irish Derby, a fourteenth victory in the race for trainer Aidan O'Brien, and a fourth for rider Seamie Heffernan.

Opposite bottom: *Serpentine* and Emmet McNamara have led from flagfall and are still clear in the Epsom Derby, to record a record-breaking eighth victory in the Blue Riband race for the colt's trainer Aidan O'Brien.

Opposite: Rider Colin Keane returns on *Even So* with Shane Lyons, brother and assistant trainer to the filly's trainer Ger, after they have landed the Irish Oaks at The Curragh.

Bottom: The Ado McGuinness-trained *Saltonstall* (near side) gets up in the dying strides under Gavin Ryan to snatch the Colm Quinn BMW Mile from *Njord* and Tom Madden. Deliberations over the photo finish took so long that a dead-heat appeared to be inevitable but, in the end, the photographic evidence revealed that *Saltonstall* had got home by a pixel.

The Donnacha O'Brien-trained *Fancy Blue* (near side) gets home by a neck under Ryan Moore from *One Voice* and Tom Marquand (yellow cap) in the Nassau Stakes at Goodwood. It was a second Group 1 win for the fledgling trainer, just three weeks after he had claimed his first when *Fancy Blue* won the Prix de Diane at Longchamp.

Lucky Vega goes clear under Shane Foley, the Jessica Harrington-trained colt putting up a really impressive performance in landing the Phoenix Stakes at The Curragh.

Trainer Tony Mullins congratulates rider Joey Sheridan as he is led in by groom
Jackie Carter to Galway's winner's enclosure, having won the Listed Oyster
Stakes on *Princess Zoe*. It was a fourth win in a row for Paddy Kehoe's and
Philomena Crampton's remarkable mare who, the following month, won the
Group 1 Prix du Cadran at Longchamp.

The Joseph O'Brien-trained *Galileo Chrome* stays on strongly for Tom Marquand (red and yellow hooped cap) to get the better of *Berkshire Rocco* and Andrea Atzeni (red cap) and land the St Leger at Doncaster, with the Irish Derby winner *Santiago* and Frankie Dettori (blue and orange striped cap) back in fourth.

It's thumbs-up from trainer Johnny Murtagh in Leopardstown's
winner's enclosure with *Champers Elysees* and groom Ryan
McKeever, after the filly, ridden by Colin Keane, has landed the
Matron Stakes, and provided Johnny Murtagh with his first Group 1
win as a trainer.

Search For A Song stays on best of all for Oisín Orr (near side) to get
home by two lengths from *Fujaira Prince* (number 2) and *Twilight Payment*
(far side) and land her second Irish St Leger. It was a first Group 1
win for rider Oisín Orr and it was a ninth win in the race for trainer
Dermot Weld, which equalled Dr Vincent O'Brien's record.

Well spaced out at The Curragh on Irish Champions' Weekend, behind closed doors during Covid-19.

Trainer Joseph O'Brien and rider Shane Crosse on the winners' podium at
Newmarket after *Pretty Gorgeous*'s victory in the Fillies' Mile. It was a first Group 1
win for the rider, and it was no more than he deserved, a month after he had missed
out on the winning ride on *Galileo Chrome* in the St Leger at Doncaster after testing
positive for Covid-19.

The Jim Bolger-trained *Mac Swiney* stays on strongly for Kevin Manning to land the Vertem Futurity Trophy at Doncaster. The horse was named after Terence MacSwiney, Irish author and politician, whose 100th anniversary was the day before the race.

Twilight Payment under Jye McNeil gets home by a half a length from *Tiger Moth* in the Melbourne Cup, with *Prince Of Arran* just a head back in third place. It was a second Melbourne Cup win for trainer Joseph O'Brien, three years after he won his first with *Rekindling*.

They're off in the Breeders' Cup Mile at Keeneland, a race that is won by *Order Of Australia* (far right, number 15) and Pierre-Charles Boudot, with *Circus Maximus* (far left) and Ryan Moore finishing second and *Lope Y Fernandez* (third from left, number 3) and Frankie Dettori finishing third. It was a first victory in the Breeders' Cup Mile for trainer Aidan O'Brien, who was responsible for the second and third too for good measure.

Tarnawa goes clear for Colin Keane to post an impressive victory in the Breeders'
Cup Turf. It was a first win in the Breeders' Cup Turf for trainer Dermot Weld and
a first Breeders' Cup win for rider Colin Keane, who stepped in for the ride after
Christophe Soumillon had tested positive for Covid-19.

Trainer John Oxx at work at Currabeg Stables. John Oxx was at the top of his profession as a racehorse trainer for decades, from *Eurobird*'s win in the 1987 Irish St Leger, through *Ridgewood Pearl*, *Timarida*, *Sinndar*, *Alamshar* and *Azamour*. His best horse, however, was *Sea The Stars*, who won six Group 1 races in six months in 2009, one every month, including the 2000 Guineas (**opposite**) with jockey Michael Kinane on board, The Derby and the Eclipse, before he rounded off his season and his racing career with a famous victory in the Prix de l'Arc de Triomphe at Longchamp. John Oxx retired as a racehorse trainer in 2020.

2021

The Jim Bolger-trained
Poetic Flare and Kevin
Manning are clear in the
St James's Palace Stakes at
Royal Ascot

Grooms Ger Flynn (left) and John Griffin (right) congratulate Rory
Cleary and the Jim-Bolger trained *Mac Swiney* as they return after
landing the Tattersalls Irish 2000 Guineas at The Curragh.

A kiss for the Aidan O'Brien-trained *Empress Josephine*
after she and rider Seamie Heffernan have teamed up
to win the Tattersalls Irish 1000 Guineas.

Snowfall and Frankie Dettori (left, purple cap) come clear in the Cazoo Oaks at Epsom and coast to a record-breaking sixteen-length success.

Trainer Gavin Cromwell congratulates rider Gary Carroll
as he and *Quick Suzy* make their way back to the winner's
enclosure at Royal Ascot, with groom Becky Rafter, after
winning the Queen Mary Stakes – a first Royal Ascot win
for both jockey and trainer.

The Aidan O'Brien-trained *Love* and rider Ryan Moore with connections in the winner's enclosure after they have won the Prince of Wales's Stakes at Royal Ascot.

Johnny Murtagh in the winner's enclosure with his wife, Orla, and *Create Belief* after victory in the Sandringham Handicap. Johnny Murtagh won forty-eight races at Royal Ascot as a jockey. This was his first win there as a trainer.

Trainer Willie Mullins celebrates after *Stratum* has won
the Queen Alexandra Stakes at Royal Ascot.

Frankie Dettori (right, orange cap) on *Lone Eagle* congratulates
William Buick (blue silks) on *Hurricane Lane* as the pair of them pull
up after *Hurricane Lane* has just got up to beat *Lone Eagle* by
a neck in a thrilling Dubai Duty Free Irish Derby at The Curragh.

Rider Cian MacRedmond gets a high-five from James Dooley, of part-owners
Dooley Thoroughbreds, as he returns to the winner's enclosure on the Ado
McGuinness-trained *Current Option*, led in by groom Tadhg McGuinness, after
landing the Irish Stallion Farms EBF 'Ahonoora' Handicap, the feature race on the
seventh and final day of the Galway Festival.

Members of Dooley Thoroughbreds, owners of *Sirjack Thomas*, in the winner's enclosure at Galway after their horse has won the Colm Quinn BMW Mile: Mark, Anastasia, James, Kerry, Angela, Andrea and Dave.

The Ado McGuinness-trained *Sirjack Thomas* (grey horse, third from right) makes his ground under Mikey Sheehy as they round the home turn on their way to winning the Colm Quinn BMW Mile at Galway. It was a third win in the race in three years for trainer Ado McGuinness and for owners Dooley Thoroughbreds, after *Saltonstall* (seen here in cheekpieces in front, third from left) had won it in 2019 and 2020.